C000115844

The ID16™© Personality Types series
by Jaroslaw Jankowski

The Administrator. Your Guide to the ESTJ Personality Type

The Advocate. Your Guide to the ESFJ Personality Type

The Animator. Your Guide to the ESTP Personality Type

The Artist. Your Guide to the ISFP Personality Type

The Counsellor. Your Guide to the ENFJ Personality Type

The Director. Your Guide to the ENTJ Personality Type

The Enthusiast. Your Guide to the ENFP Personality Type

The Idealist. Your Guide to the INFP Personality Type

The Innovator. Your Guide to the ENTP Personality Type

The Inspector. Your Guide to the ISTJ Personality Type

The Logician. Your Guide to the INTP Personality Type

The Mentor. Your Guide to the INFJ Personality Type

The Practitioner. Your Guide to the ISTP Personality Type

The Presenter. Your Guide to the ESFP Personality Type

The Protector. Your Guide to the ISFJ Personality Type

The Strategist. Your Guide to the INTJ Personality Type

Who Are You?

The ID16™© Personality Test

JAROSLAW JANKOWSKI
M.Ed., EMBA

This is a book which can help you exploit your potential more fully, build healthy relationships with other people and make the right decisions about your education and career. However, it should not be considered to be a substitute for expert physiological or psychiatric consultation. Neither the author nor the publisher accept any responsibility whatsoever for any detrimental effects which may result from the inappropriate use of this book.

ID16™© is an independent typology developed by Polish educator and manager Jaroslaw Jankowski and grounded in Carl Gustav Jung's theory. It should not be confused with the personality typologies and tests proposed by other authors or offered by other institutions.

Original title: Kim jesteś?
Translated from the Polish by Caryl Swift
Proof reading: Lacrosse | experts in translation
Layout editing by Zbigniew Szalbot
Cover photographs by Shutterstock

Published by LOGOS MEDIA

© Jaroslaw Jankowski 2016
All rights reserved

Paperback: ISBN 978-83-7981-096-3 .
EPUB: ISBN 978-83-7981-097-0
MOBI: ISBN 978-83-7981-098-7

Contents

Preface

It was with the dawn of history that thinkers, philosophers and common-or-garden observers of life first became interested in the phenomenon of the human personality. What intrigued them was the way that some people display a marked similarity in their behaviour and attitudes despite their very different life stories and often disparate upbringings.

Observing this, the thoughts of many turned to reflections upon types of personality. One of the fruits of these musings which remains popular to this day is the typology devised by Hippocrates. That remarkable doctor and thinker of ancient times distinguished four fundamental temperaments; the sanguine, the choleric, the phlegmatic and the melancholic. History has seen many another, equally interesting endeavour to identify and describe recurring personality types. Although some of those attempts may seem oversimplified when viewed from a contemporary perspective, they played an extraordinarily important role in their time, paving the way for subsequent, more extensive cogitations on the human personality.

The theory developed by Carl Gustav Jung (1875-1961), a Swiss psychiatrist and psychologist, came as a breakthrough in the field. It was instrumental in popularising the notion of personality types and, as of the twentieth century, it became the foundation both for the formulation of what is now known as Jungian typology and for creating personality tests grounded in that typology, the ID16™© test being a case in point.

Nowadays, personality typologies drawing on Jung's theory are widely used in teaching, training, coaching and human resource management, as well as in career and relationship counselling. They also form a basis for numerous programmes geared towards supporting personal development and improving interpersonal relationships. The majority of global businesses employ Jungian personality tests as a standard tool in their recruitment and vocational development processes. This practice was initially applied primarily in corporations of American origin; however, in recent years, it has been enjoying a steadily growing popularity in Europe as well.

Every year, thanks to Jungian personality tests, millions of people around the world are able to obtain a more profound knowledge of themselves and of others and, as a result, their lives and their relationships are changed for the better.

We sincerely hope that your exploration of personality types, with our ID16™© tools as your compass, will lead to positive transformations of exactly that kind.

ID16™© and Jungian Personality Typology

ID16™© numbers among what are referred to as Jungian personality typologies, which draw on the theories developed by Carl Gustav Jung (1875-19161), a Swiss psychiatrist and psychologist and a pioneer of the 'depth psychology' approach.

On the basis of many years of research and observation, Jung came to the conclusion that the differences in people's attitudes and preferences are far from random. He developed a concept which is highly familiar to us today: the division of people into extroverts and introverts. In addition, he distinguished four personality functions, which form two opposing pairs: sensing-intuition and thinking-feeling. He also established that one function is dominant in each pair. He became convinced that each and every person's dominant functions are fixed and independent of external conditions and that, together, what they form is a personality type.

In 1938, two American psychiatrists, Horace Gray and Joseph Wheelwright, created the first personality test based on Jung's theories. It was designed to make it possible to determine the dominant functions within the three dimensions described by Jung, namely, **extraversion-introversion**, **sensing-intuition** and **thinking-feeling**. That first test became the inspiration for other researchers. In 1942, again in America, Isabel Briggs Myers and Katherine Briggs began using their own personality test, broadening Gray's and Wheelwright's classic, three-dimensional model to include a fourth: **judging-perceiving**. The majority of subsequent personality typologies and tests drawing on Jung's theories also take that fourth dimension into account. They include the American typology published by David W. Keirsey in 1978 and the personality test developed in the nineteen seventies by Aušra Augustinavičiūtė, a Lithuanian psychologist. Over the following decades, other European researchers followed in their footsteps, creating more four-dimensional personality typologies and tests for use in personal coaching and career counselling.

ID16™© figures among that group. An independent typology developed by Polish educator and manager Jaroslaw Jankowski, it was published in the first decade of the twenty-first century. ID16™© is based on Carl Jung's classic theory and, like other contemporary Jungian typologies, it follows a four-dimensional path, terming those dimensions the **four natural inclinations**. These inclinations are dichotomous in nature and the picture they provide gives us information regarding a person's personality type. Analysis of the first inclination is intended to determine the dominant **source of life energy**, this being either the exterior or the interior world. Analysis of the second inclination defines the dominant **mode of assimilating information**, which occurs via the senses or via intuition. Analysis of the third inclination supplies a description of the **decision-making mode**, where either mind or heart is dominant, while analysis of the fourth inclination produces a definition of the dominant **lifestyle** as either organised or spontaneous. The combination of all these natural inclinations results in **sixteen possible personality types**.

One remarkable feature of the ID16™© typology is its practical dimension. It describes the individual personality types in action – at work, in daily life and in interpersonal relations. It neither concentrates on the internal dynamics of personality nor does it undertake any theoretical attempts at explaining or commenting on invisible, interior processes. The focus is turned more toward the ways in which a given personality type manifests itself externally and how it affects the surrounding world. This emphasis on the social aspect of personality places ID16™© somewhat closer to the previously mentioned typology developed by Aušra Augustinavičiūtė.

Each of the ID16™© personality types is the result of a given person's natural inclinations. There is nothing evaluative or judgemental about ascribing a person to a given type, though. No particular personality type is 'better' or 'worse' than any other. Each type is quite simply different and each has its own potential strengths and weaknesses. ID16™© makes it possible to identify and describe those differences. It helps us to understand ourselves and discover our place in the world.

Familiarity with our personality profile enables us to make full use of our potential and work on the areas which might cause us trouble. It is an invaluable aid in everyday life, in solving problems, in building healthy relationships with other people and in making decisions relating to our education and careers.

Determining personality is a process which is neither arbitrary nor mechanical in nature. As the 'owner and user' of our personality, each and every one of us is fully capable of defining which type we belong to. The individual's role is thus pivotal. This self-identification can be achieved either by analysing the descriptions of the ID16™© personality types and steadily narrowing down the fields of choice or by taking the short cut provided by the ID16™© Personality Test (see next chapter). The role played by each 'personality user' is equally crucial when it comes to the test, given that the outcome depends entirely on the answers they provide.

Identifying personality types helps us to know both ourselves and others. Nonetheless, it should not be treated as some kind of future-determining oracle. No personality type can ever justify our weaknesses or poor interpersonal relationships. It might, however, help us to understand their causes!

ID16™© treats personality type not as a static, genetic, pre-determined condition, but as a product of innate and acquired characteristics. As such, it is a concept which neither diminishes free will nor engages in pigeonholing people. What it does is open up new perspectives for us, encouraging us to work on ourselves and indicating the areas where that work is most needed.

The ID16™© Personality Test

The ID16™© Personality Test is a set of eighty-four questions concerning your reactions and behaviour in normal, everyday situations. The answers make it possible to determine your personality type.

Essential information!

- The test consists of three parts. Each part contains twenty-eight questions about your personal preferences or behaviour patterns. The questions take the form of sentences which you need to complete by choosing one of two options.
- The test is designed to determine your personality type and NOT your intelligence, knowledge or skills. The results are not in the least a value judgement! There are no 'good' or 'bad' answers and no 'right' or 'wrong' ones. So please don't try to work out which answer is 'the proper one' and choose that. Each of the ID16™© personality types

is different, but they all have the same worth. No particular personality type is 'better' or 'worse' than any other.

- Select each of the answers in line with the way *you behave* in the situation being described and NOT in the way *you would like* to behave or in the way that, in your opinion, *one ought* to behave. If you have never been in a given situation, then give some thought to what your natural reaction would be if you did find yourself in those circumstances. When a question concerns preferences, choose the answer which reflects your real inclinations and NOT the one which seems to be 'correct' or 'desirable'.

- You will need to answer *all the questions*. In the event that you can't fully identify with either of the available choices, select the one which is closer to the way you think you would react or behave.

- There is no time limit, so you don't need to rush. On the other hand, don't spend too long pondering your answers, either.

- Each of the answers is followed by a letter in brackets: E, I, S, N, T, F, J or P. As you do the test, make a note of the letter which follows the answer you've chosen. When you've answered all the questions, count how many times you chose each of the letters. As an example, your results might look like this:
    - o E: 18;
    - o I: 3;
    - o S: 7;
    - o N: 14;
    - o T: 4;
    - o F: 17;
    - o J: 0;
    - o P: 21.

- You'll find the rest of the instructions at the end of the test.

Part 1 of 3

1. I often wonder about the meaning of life:
    a. yes. [I]
    b. no. [E]
2. The solutions that appeal to me more are:
    a. tried and tested. [S]
    b. innovative and creative. [N]
3. I like working:
    a. as part of a team. [E]
    b. on my own. [I]
4. I more often:
    a. take the advice of others. [P]
    b. advise others myself. [J]
5. In order to maintain good relations with people, I often make concessions to others, even when it doesn't suit me to do so:
    a. yes. [F]
    b. no. [T]
6. I relax best when:
    a. I'm on my own or in a small group, in a quiet and peaceful spot. [I]
    b. I'm in a crowd, in a spot where something's always going on. [E]
7. I often finish a job before the deadline or do more than is strictly necessary:
    a. yes. [J]
    b. no. [P]
8. The following description fits me better:
    a. I like to have my day planned out and I'm not very keen on sudden and unexpected changes of plan. [J]
    b. I dislike rigidly planned days and view sudden changes as variety. [P]
9. When I'm in company, I normally say:
    a. more than the other people. [E]
    b. less than the other people. [I]

10. I prefer authors who:
    a. make use of interesting comparisons and invoke innovative ideas and concepts. [N]
    b. write in a sober style and focus on facts. [S]
11. When I'm solving a problem, I try, above all:
    a. to remain objective, even at the cost of being liked by people. [T]
    b. to preserve people's liking for me, even at the cost of my objectivity. [F]
12. I would rather be involved with:
    a. tasks similar to ones I've carried out before. [S]
    b. new tasks that I've never encountered before. [N]
13. When I want to sort something out and put it behind me, I often make decisions prematurely:
    a. yes. [J]
    b. no. [P]
14. The following description fits me better:
    a. I'm capable of concentrating on one thing for a long time. [I]
    b. I'm easily distracted and often break off what I'm doing. [E]
15. I'm more irritated by:
    a. dreamers who mainly think about the future. [S]
    b. realists who are interested in the here and now. [N]
16. I'd rather attend classes or training sessions given by lecturers or instructors who are:
    a. cold and sometimes discourteous, but highly logical, conveying their knowledge in an orderly fashion. [T]
    b. vague, with a rather chaotic teaching style, but really likeable and warm-hearted. [F]

17. When I have to do something within a fixed time limit, I usually:
    a. try to get the job done as fast as I can, so that I can turn to more pleasant things. [J]
    b. deal with more pleasant things first and only get down to the job when the deadline is looming. [P]
18. I believe that:
    a. objective and warranted criticism is desirable in the majority of situations and that it helps people to perceive their oversights and errors. [T]
    b. criticism, even when it's objective and warranted, often does more harm than good, since it damages interpersonal relations. [F]
19. I like to make a note of the dates and times of future meetings and get-togethers, trips and matters that need sorting out:
    a. yes. [J]
    b. no. [P]
20. I often wonder whether what people say contains hidden allusions or comments directed at me:
    a. yes. [F]
    b. no. [T]
21. If I were investing my savings, I'd prefer:
    a. a higher profit earned over a longer period of time. [N]
    b. a lower but faster profit. [S]
22. I'd rather:
    a. learn new things. [N]
    b. improve my current skills. [S]
23. I'm more irritated by people who:
    a. are poor organisers and lack any predilection for order. [J]
    b. are too inflexible and can't adapt readily to new circumstances. [P]

24. I believe that it's worse to:
    a. treat people unjustly. [T]
    b. lack understanding for people who find themselves in a difficult situation. [F]
25. I more often regret:
    a. saying too much. [E]
    b. saying too little. [I]
26. When I'm carrying out a task, I usually:
    a. split it into smaller parts and work on them steadily, systematically pressing on with the job. [S]
    b. I have moments when the ideas flow and moments of intensive work and thanks to that I move ahead with the job. [N]
27. I often wonder why people:
    a. don't think about others. [F]
    b. behave illogically. [T]
28. I find it hard to put up with:
    a. hubbub, confusion and the presence of large numbers of people. [I]
    b. quietness, boredom and solitariness. [E]

Part 2 of 3

1. I feel more comfortable psychologically when:
    a. I still haven't made a final decision and have room to manoeuvre. [P]
    b. I've made a final decision and the matter is closed. [J]
2. I'm normally one of the first to phone and comfort someone who's in a difficult situation:
    a. yes. [F]
    b. no. [T]
3. I'm often moved when I see reports about people who have met with misfortune:
    a. yes. [F]
    b. no. [T]

4. When I'm beginning a job:
    a. I often prepare a plan of action or list what needs to be done. [J]
    b. I don't usually waste time on drawing up a plan of action, but get to work straight away. [P]

5. When I want to learn how to use a new device, I usually:
    a. read the instructions carefully first and only then try starting it up. [S]
    b. have a look at it and then start it up, only having a look at the instructions if there's a problem. [N]

6. Once I've completed a task, I get more satisfaction from:
    a. my own awareness that I've done a good job. [T]
    b. praise and recognition from other people. [F]

7. I often tell others about my experiences:
    a. yes. [E]
    b. no. [I]

8. I usually act:
    a. impulsively. [P]
    b. after deliberation. [J]

9. When I'm working in a group of people, I prefer it if:
    a. minor disagreements and conflicts occur within the group, just as long as there are clear and transparent rules in place. [T]
    b. there are no clear and transparent rules within the group, just as long as a good, friendly atmosphere prevails. [F]

10. I'd rather do a job which demands:
    a. imagination and the ability to predict. [N]
    b. adherence to a number of detailed procedures. [S]

11. I often wonder what the future will bring:
    a. yes. [N]
    b. no. [S]
12. I prefer tasks which:
    a. require me to work by myself. [I]
    b. require contact with people. [E]
13. I like watching programmes:
    a. which present original theories and stimulate the imagination. [N]
    b. are of the 'how-to' ilk and proffer instructions which can be put into practice. [S]
14. I often interrupt people while they're speaking:
    a. yes. [E]
    b. no. [I]
15. I prefer people whose decision-making is guided by:
    a. internal conviction and fellow-feeling or compassion for others. [F]
    b. logic and an objective analysis of the situation. [T]
16. I like:
    a. playing a major role. [E]
    b. operating in the background. [I]
17. I more often:
    a. listen to the opinions and viewpoints of other people. [P]
    b. present my viewpoints and opinions to others. [J]
18. I believe that it is worse:
    a. to be overly critical. [F]
    b. to be overly lenient. [T]
19. I often make a note of the things I have to do during a given day:
    a. yes. [J]
    b. no. [P]

20. When I'm given a larger task to perform, I'd rather:
    a. receive concrete instructions explaining how I should do it. [S]
    b. have the opportunity of doing it in line with my own ideas. [N]
21. When I'm discussing a problem that needs solving with others, I usually:
    a. start by considering the issue in question and only enter the discussion once I have an idea. [I]
    b. enter the discussion spontaneously, with new ideas coming into my mind as we talk. [E]
22. Conflict resolution depends first and foremost on:
    a. calming the situation down and achieving a compromise. [F]
    b. clarifying who was in the right and who was in the wrong. [T]
23. When I'm asked about something, I usually:
    a. reply at once. [E]
    b. need a moment to think. [I]
24. When I'm solving a problem, I'm capable of:
    a. seeing the wider context of the issue in question and predicting its consequences. [N]
    b. focusing on all the details concerning the issue in question. [S]
25. When I have a task to do, I usually:
    a. put off finishing it, so as to have the chance to make any changes which might be needed. [P]
    b. try to finish it as quickly as possible, so that it's over and done with. [J]
26. I'd rather work with people who are:
    a. practical, precise and meticulous. [S]
    b. creative, inventive and resourceful. [N]

27. My mood and emotional state are usually:
    a. difficult to discern. [I]
    b. easy to discern. [E]
28. Some people would judge me to be:
    a. disorganised. [P]
    b. too inflexible. [J]

Part 3 of 3

1. I prefer people who:
    a. are capable of thinking logically. [T]
    b. are able to empathise with other people's situations. [F]
2. I like:
    a. a life full of changes and surprises. [P]
    b. a well-ordered life where everything happens according to plan. [J]
3. When I'm in a large group, I usually:
    a. talk to a handful of people, mainly those I already know. [I]
    b. talk to a lot of people, including those I don't know. [E]
4. I'd be more bored meeting someone who:
    a. proffers huge amounts of detailed information and asks a great many practical questions. [N]
    b. floats a sweeping vision of new solutions, but one devoid of details. [S]
5. A decision is worse when:
    a. it's illogical. [T]
    b. it brings harm to a large number of people. [F]
6. Others would judge me to be reserved and say that I rarely show my emotions:
    a. yes. [I]
    b. no. [E]

7. When I'm on holiday, I often plan what I'm going to do the next day in advance:
   a. yes. [J]
   b. no. [P]
8. I'd rather be praised because:
   a. it's pleasant spending time with me. [F]
   b. I'm capable of making the right decisions. [T]
9. I prefer:
   a. solitary walks. [I]
   b. meeting new people. [E]
10. Others would judge me to be someone who:
    a. acts as previously planned. [J]
    b. acts spontaneously. [P]
11. If I'm looking for a job, my main focus is on:
    a. the terms and conditions of employment on offer. [S]
    b. the future potential of the position in question. [N]
12. The following description fits me better:
    a. I frequently fail to be prepared in time and get myself out of trouble by improvising. [P]
    b. I'm normally well-prepared and I don't need to improvise. [J]
13. Being amongst people normally:
    a. drains me. [I]
    b. gives me an added boost. [E]
14. I feel uneasy when I'm the centre of attention:
    a. yes. [I]
    b. no. [E]
15. The following description fits me better:
    a. I'm often late when I've arranged to meet someone. [P]
    b. when I've arranged to meet someone, I generally arrive punctually or early. [J]

16. If I'm searching for someone to collaborate with, my main focus is on:
    a. whether our personalities are suited and we'll be able to work together harmoniously. [F]
    b. if a given person has the necessary qualifications and abilities for the tasks in question. [T]

17. Others would say that I'm:
    a. practical. [S]
    b. ingenious. [N]

18. When I'm listening to other people's problems:
    a. I often wonder what their objective cause was and whether the person concerned wasn't responsible for the current state of affairs. [T]
    b. I usually feel a heartfelt sympathy for them and wonder how I can help them. [F]

19. I'm more interested in:
    a. people's actual behaviour and real events. [S]
    b. the general principles driving people's behaviour and events. [N]

20. When criticising other people, the most crucial thing is:
    a. to remain objective. [T]
    b. to take care not to hurt their feelings. [F]

21. A pleasant weekend is one spent:
    a. relaxing at home with a good book or film. [I]
    b. meeting friends, talking or enjoying ourselves together. [E]

22. I get more joy from:
    a. finishing work on a task. [J]
    b. beginning work on a new task. [P]

23. Established procedures, instructions and guidelines:
    a. are usually a practical aid and make the job easier. [S]
    b. often restrict creative ideas and make the job more difficult. [N]

24. I often put off making a decision, wanting to gather more and more information or think things over:
    a. yes. [P]
    b. no. [J]

25. When I hear about an unusual venture, I'm usually:
    a. fascinated by the idea or concept itself. [N]
    b. interested in the way it was or is being accomplished. [S]

26. The following description fits me better:
    a. I'm reluctant to make adverse comments to others and, if I have to, then I do it tactfully. [F]
    b. I'm direct; if I don't like something, then I'll say so. [T]

27. I'd rather work:
    a. by myself or with two close colleagues. [I]
    b. in a new, ten-person team. [E]

28. Once I've completed a form or questionnaire, then I usually go back and check that I've filled in all the details or answers properly:
    a. yes. [S]
    b. no. [N]

And that's it … the end of the test! Now it's time to interpret the results.

Step 1

Check how often you've selected answers followed by each of the letters: E, I, S, N, T, F, J or P.

As an example, your results might look like this:

- E: 18;
- I: 3;
- S: 7;
- N: 14;
- T: 4;
- F: 17;
- J: 0;
- P: 21.

Step 2

Below, you'll find the letters arranged as four sets of pairs. For each pair, select the letter you chose more often and make a note of it:

Pair 1: **E** or **I**;

Pair 2: **S** or **N**;

Pair 3: **T** or **F**;

Pair 4: **J** or **P**.

Your result will now take the form of a four-letter 'code'; in our example, it's **ENFP**.

The higher number in each of the pairs stands for the dominant inclination in the respective dimension of the personality:

- Source of life energy: E, the exterior world or I, the interior world;
- Mode of assimilating information: S, via the senses or N, via intuition;

- Decision-making mode: T, with the mind or F, with the heart;
- Lifestyle: J, which is organised or P, which is spontaneous.

Step 3

Now find your four-letter 'code' on the list below and check out your personality type!

- ENFJ: the Counsellor (see p. 41)
- ENFP: the Enthusiast (see p. 49)
- ENTJ: the Director (see p. 45)
- ENTP: the Innovator (see p. 56)
- ESFJ: the Advocate (see p. 32)
- ESFP: the Presenter (see p. 70)
- ESTJ: the Administrator (see p. 29)
- ESTP: the Animator (see p. 35)
- INFJ: the Mentor (see p. 64)
- INFP: the Idealist (see p. 52)
- INTJ: the Strategist (see p. 77)
- INTP: the Logician (see p. 61)
- ISFJ: the Protector (see p. 74)
- ISFP: the Artist (see p. 38)
- ISTJ: the Inspector (see p. 59)
- ISTP: the Practitioner (see p. 67)

The ID16™© Personality Types

The Administrator (ESTJ)

Life motto: *We'll get the job done!*

Administrators are hard-working, responsible and extremely loyal. Energetic and decisive, they value order, stability, security and clear rules. They are matter-of-fact and businesslike, logical, rational and practical and possess the capability to assimilate large amounts of detailed information.

Superb organisers, they are intolerant of ineffectuality, wastefulness and slothfulness. True to their convictions and direct in their contact with others, they present their point of view decisively and openly express critical opinions, sometimes hurting other people as a result.

The *administrator's* four natural inclinations:

- source of life energy: the exterior world
- mode of assimilating information: via the senses
- decision-making mode: the mind
- lifestyle: organised

Potential strengths

Administrators are enthusiastic, friendly and ready to extend a helping hand to others. In terms of their work, they are self-motivating and have a sense of duty. Energetic, decisive and matter-of-fact, they are happy to accept responsibility for accomplishing tasks. With their natural leadership skills, they are capable of heading up teams and supervising others. They are able to evaluate impartially and objectively and are logical, rational and practical. They will always speak their mind and are direct in their contact with others, accept criticism well and are also capable of carrying out critical appraisals.

As a rule, they are highly perceptive, have good memories and are able to assimilate large amounts of detailed information. When they can see the potential for streamlining a system, improving its effectiveness and efficiency or putting a stop to waste, they feel stirred to take action. Capable when it comes to drawing up plans and establishing procedures, they will spot flaws and shortcomings imperceptible to others. They are hard-working, responsible and extremely loyal and complete the jobs they are given on time or, indeed, quite often before the deadline. They are incapable of consciously working to less than their full potential. With their love of order and organisational flair, they are excellent and capable resource managers and superb system organisers and administrators. Characterised by their independence and resistance to manipulation, they are true to their convictions and, no matter what the prevailing opinion might be, they stick to their own principles.

Potential weaknesses

As a rule, *administrators* assume that they are right. They will often shut out points of view which differ from their own, and as a result they narrow their own field of perception. With their natural inclination to instruct and advise, they will sometimes behave condescendingly and try to exert pressure on others. They have a tendency to focus excessively on details, which often means that they fail to perceive the bigger picture. Digesting theories and predicting the future consequences of present decisions and events comes hard to them. They feel that they are on very uncertain ground in situations which demand that they think ahead into the future or rely on intuition or improvisation. They have an inclination to concentrate on urgent tasks at the expense of important ones. Two problems that frequently crop up are their failure to delegate sufficiently and their habit of interfering in the work of their subordinates or colleagues. They are highly demanding, their expectations can be unrealistic and they can give the impression of being almost impossible to satisfy.

Reading the emotions and feelings of others is difficult for them, which often means that they unwittingly upset people. They have little awareness of the fact that their bluntly expressed opinions and jokes might be hurtful to others. Their mode of communication may not always be appropriate to the situation and circumstances in which they find themselves. Expressing their own emotions and demonstrating warmth towards others is also hard for them. In general, they are sparing in their praise and generous with their criticism. Being somewhat inflexible by nature, they find it difficult to cope with change. They can be stubborn, dogmatic, impatient and irritable and may be overly focused on immediate benefits, social status and material possessions.

Similar personality types:

- the Animator
- the Inspector
- the Practitioner

Statistical data:

- *administrators* constitute between ten and thirteen per cent of the global community
- men predominate among *administrators* (60 per cent)
- the United States is an example of a nation corresponding to the *administrator's* profile[1]

Find out more!

The Administrator. Your Guide to the ESTJ Personality Type by Jaroslaw Jankowski

The Advocate (ESFJ)

Life motto: *How can I help you?*

Advocates are well-organised, energetic and enthusiastic. Practical, responsible and conscientious, they are sincere and exceptionally gregarious.

Advocates are perceptive of human feelings, emotions and needs. They value harmony and find criticism and conflict difficult to bear. With their sensitivity to any and every manifestation of injustice, prejudice or detriment to another, they are genuinely interested in other people's problems and take real delight in helping them and tending

---

[1] What this means is not that all the residents of the USA fall within this personality type, but that American society as a whole possesses a great many of the character traits typical of the *administrator*.

to their needs, while often neglecting their own. They have a tendency to do everything for others and can be vulnerable to manipulation.

The *advocate*'s four natural inclinations:

- source of life energy: the exterior world
- mode of assimilating information: via the senses
- decision-making mode: the heart
- lifestyle: organised

Potential strengths

Advocates like people and are genuinely interested in their experiences and problems. Being highly empathic, they are capable of reading the feelings and emotions of others, and are equally as good at expressing their own. Their warm, sincere interest and solicitude draws other people to them. They create a healthy, friendly atmosphere around themselves and excel when working as part of a group. They are also superb organisers, capable of turning their efforts to common goals. Gifted with the ability to collaborate harmoniously, they take genuine delight in the success of others and, as a motivating force, give other people faith in their own powers and elicit their hidden potential.

They are loyal employees, more focused on accomplishing the tasks entrusted to them than on personal benefits, which is why they are less likely than others to change jobs in search of better terms and conditions. By nature hard-working, energetic and stable, *advocates* are also characterised by their realism, pragmatism and predictability. What interests them are concrete facts and they are attracted by effective and practical solutions which either eliminate real problems or make someone's life easier.

They will finish what they start. Entrust a job to them and, rest assured, they will engage to the utmost in accomplishing it. *Advocates* cope well with tasks which require adherence to strict procedures, involve large amounts of data and demand repetitive activities.

Potential weaknesses

Being oriented towards helping others and low on assertiveness means that *advocates* are not always very good at tending to their own needs or defending their own interests and are also vulnerable to deceit, manipulation and emotional blackmail. They have a tendency to avoid difficult conversations, even when they are essential. Incapable of ending toxic and damaging relationships, they are inclined to blame themselves for any failure in that area of their lives. They fare poorly when dealing with crises and are extremely sensitive to criticism. Working alone comes hard to them and they are dependent on praise and affirmation from other people. When faced with hostility or indifference, they may well lose faith in themselves.

They find it difficult to cope in fields of activity which are completely new to them and are attached to old, tried and tested solutions, which might cause them to regard experiments and innovative methods of operating with scepticism. Being rather inflexible, they rapidly find themselves completely at sea in situations demanding swift decisions and improvisation. They also have a problem with delegating duties and responsibilities, as well as a tendency to do too much for others and help them whether they like it or not. Despite their tremendous openness to people, *advocates* are often sceptical when it comes to points of view other than their own. Indeed, simply encountering those opinions can cause them a deep sense of unease. They are also inclined to negate and reject the new and unfamiliar prematurely and, more often than most, are characterised by dogmatism and an inability to perceive the complexity of events.

Their loyalty towards people can bias them and they have difficulty in accepting that their relatives, friends or colleagues might be in the wrong or at fault. With their focus on current needs, *advocates* may not perceive future challenges and, in concentrating on individual problems, might fail to take note of the wider context.

Similar personality types:

- the Presenter
- the Protector
- the Artist

Statistical data:

- *advocates* constitute between ten and thirteen per cent of the global community
- women predominate among *advocates* (70 per cent)
- Canada is an example of a nation corresponding to the *advocate's* profile[2]

Find out more!

The Advocate. Your Guide to the ESFJ Personality Type by Jaroslaw Jankowski

The Animator (ESTP)

Life motto: *Let's DO something!*

Animators are energetic, active and enterprising. Fond of the company of others, they have the ability to enjoy the moment and are spontaneous, flexible and open to change.

Animators are inspirers and instigators, spurring others to act. Being logical, rational and pragmatic realists, they are

---

[2] What this means is not that all the residents of Canada fall within this personality type, but that Canadian society as a whole possesses a great many of the character traits typical of the *advocate*.

wearied by abstract concepts and solutions for the future. Their focus is on solving concrete problems in the here and now. They have difficulties with organising and planning and can be impulsive, acting first and thinking later.

The *animator's* four natural inclinations:

- source of life energy: the exterior world
- mode of assimilating information: via the senses
- decision-making mode: the mind
- lifestyle: spontaneous

Potential strengths

Animators are open, optimistic and quick to establish contact with others. They hold no grudges, but are able to forgive both other people and themselves. They live for today, enjoying the here and now and not tormenting themselves with thoughts of past mistakes. Splendid observers, with excellent memories, they are characterised by their uncommon flexibility and spontaneity, find change easy to handle and adapt rapidly to new circumstances. Being unusually logical and rational, they enjoy tackling practical problems and have no fear of 'insoluble' tasks. They have the ability to size up a situation rapidly and, with their extraordinary gift for improvisation, to respond appropriately to problems and changing circumstances as they crop up. Efficient, enterprising and energetic, they cope well in situations of conflict, are impervious to criticism and, when convinced that they should take a particular action, they are capable of doing so regardless of the views and opinions of others. Dissuading them is something of a challenge.

By nature bold and unafraid of risk, *animators* infect others with their enthusiasm and faith that their undertakings will succeed. They initiate all kinds of activities and motivate others to work. Capable of investing their entire energy in a task that matters to them, they are just as good at relaxing. As a rule, they are superb oral communicators, keeping their listeners riveted with their colourful, witty and fascinating way with the spoken word. They also possess the gift of persuasiveness.

Potential weaknesses

Animators have a problem with defining priorities and with operating methodically and systematically, being prone to act impulsively. Their activities are usually reactions to immediate problems and challenges; they will rarely be the result of planned actions taken with the future in mind. Focused as they are on the here and now, they have trouble identifying future opportunities and threats, as well as with foreseeing the consequences of their actions and their impact on other people. They are easily distracted. When they catch sight of a new challenge, their enthusiasm for things they have already started doing dissolves and, as a result, they have problems with keeping their promises and seeing things through to the end. Their poor planning and time management skills can sometimes mean that they fail to organise their tasks properly, missing deadlines as a consequence.

Animators cope badly with tasks requiring them to work alone and demanding lengthy preparation by way of reading large amounts of material, for instance, or drawing up a detailed plan of action. In general, they do no better when it comes to routine tasks and repetitive activities and anything which entails abstract thinking or looking ahead to the future will also be a problem for them. By nature impatient and quick to tire of situations, they are also frequently characterised by an inclination towards risk and dicing with danger. Their self-assurance usually helps them to succeed; however, on occasion, it can lead them to overestimate their capabilities or underrate the seriousness of a problem. Despite their excellent interpersonal relationships in the social sphere, *animators* have difficulty both in reading the emotions and feelings of others and in expressing their own. It can happen that they hurt other people with their explicit or critical remarks, while they themselves remain completely unaware of the impact of their words.

Similar personality types:

- the Administrator
- the Practitioner
- the Inspector

Statistical data:

- *animators* constitute between six and ten per cent of the global community
- men predominate among *animators* (60 per cent)
- Australia is an example of a nation corresponding to the *animator's* profile[3]

Find out more!

The Animator. Your Guide to the ESTP Personality Type by Jaroslaw Jankowski

The Artist (ISFP)

Life motto: *Let's create something!*

Artists are sensitive, creative and original, with a sense of the aesthetic and natural artistic talents. Independent in character, they follow their own system of values and are

---

[3] What this means is not that all the residents of Australia fall within this personality type, but that Australian society as a whole possesses a great many of the character traits typical of the *animator*.

optimistic in outlook, with a positive approach to life and an ability to enjoy the moment.

Helping others is a source of joy to them. They find abstract theories tedious and would rather create reality than talk about it, although starting on something new comes more easily to them than finishing what they have already started. They have difficulty in voicing their own desires and needs.

The *artist's* four natural inclinations:

- source of life energy: the interior world
- mode of assimilating information: via the senses
- decision-making mode: the heart
- lifestyle: spontaneous

Potential strengths

Artists are optimistic by nature, with a positive approach to life. They are exceptionally sincere and are characterised by their openness to people and their tolerance. Being aesthetically inclined, they have a feel for beauty, an artistic spirit and a superb sense of space, colour, hues and sounds, as well as the ability to take whatever tools and materials are available to them and use them to create stunning compositions, images and objects. They are quicker than most to spot new trends in fashion, design and art. When they are working on tasks they believe in, they are capable of investing enormous effort and energy in them. They learn fast by doing. *Artists* are genuine altruists; they take a sincere interest in other people's experiences and problems and long to help them. They are able to show others warmth and care and respect their individualism. Superb listeners, they will find a positive potential and good in everyone.

With their uncanny gift for empathy, they are able to help other people, giving them heart and faith in their own powers. They are independent, following their own system of values and remaining insusceptible to pressure.

Speculations about the future fail to absorb them and worrying over past mistakes is alien to them; they have the ability to focus absolutely on immediate and current problems. Being highly flexible, they find change easy to handle and adapt rapidly to new circumstances, responding to them quickly. They know how to make the most of a situation's potential and, when the need arises, they can improvise brilliantly.

Potential weaknesses

As a rule, *artists* cope none too well with tasks stretching over a lengthy time span and demanding planning, preparation and thinking ahead. Motivating them to do jobs where the results will only become apparent at some distant moment in time is a challenging undertaking. They have a tendency to act and make decisions impulsively and are better at starting something new than at finishing what they have already begun. Analytic and rational decision-making in detachment from real people and situations is difficult for them. In general, they evaluate themselves through the prism of other people's views and assessments of them; by the same token, they are highly sensitive and easily hurt. This might give rise to major problems in the lives of *artists* who are operating in an environment hostile to their nature, for instance among people who are very sparing in their praise or generous in their criticism. They are inclined to have low self-esteem and it is all too easy to undermine their faith in themselves. Openly voicing their thoughts and desires is something they often dread.

Artists have a very low tolerance threshold when it comes to being criticised and may perceive criticism even where none is intended; they are also liable to take opinions which run contrary to their own as an attack on their system of values. This can lead to their shutting out information at variance with their views and limiting their own perceptions as a result. They frequently have problems with assimilating theories and grasping concepts unsuited to practical application. Their individualism and fondness for doing things 'their way' hampers them when it comes to teamwork. When carrying out management functions, they have difficulty in disciplining people, calling their attention to poor achievements, giving instructions and enforcing duties.

Similar personality types:

- the Protector
- the Presenter
- the Advocate

Statistical data:

- *artists* constitute between six and nine per cent of the global community
- women predominate among *artists* (60 per cent)
- China is an example of a nation corresponding to the *artist's* profile[4]

Find out more!

The Artist. Your Guide to the ISFP Personality Type by Jaroslaw Jankowski

The Counsellor (ENFJ)

Life motto: *My friends are my world*

Counsellors are optimistic, enthusiastic and quick-witted. Courteous and tactful, they have an extraordinary gift for empathy and find joy in acting for the good of others, with

---

[4] What this means is not that all the residents of China fall within this personality type, but that Chinese society as a whole possesses a great many of the character traits typical of the *artist*.

no thought of themselves. They have the ability to influence other people, inspiring them, eliciting their hidden potential and giving them faith in their own powers. Radiating warmth, they draw others to them and often help them in solving their personal problems.

Counsellors can be over-trusting and have a tendency to view the world through rose-tinted glasses. With their focus on other people, they often forget about their own needs.

The *counsellor's* four natural inclinations:

- source of life energy: the exterior world
- mode of assimilating information: intuition
- decision-making mode: the heart
- lifestyle: organised

Potential strengths

Counsellors are energetic and optimistic. Loyal and faithful, they can always be relied on. They are conscientious, responsible, orderly and well-organised. Their thinking is global and far-reaching and they look at problems from a broad perspective, perceiving various aspects of the issues they are engaging with. They live in accordance with the values they profess and, when the situation demands, they will stand in their defence without regard for the consequences. They voice their feelings and emotions openly and have excellent oral skills, with the ability to express their thoughts intelligibly and persuasively. However, imposing their views on others is alien to them, as is making themselves the focal point. Their focus is on other people; *counsellors* give of their time unstintingly and are ready to adapt to others and their needs if doing so will enable them to provide help in solving their problems or changing their lives for the better.

They display extraordinary tact and intuition in their interpersonal communication and are masters of the diplomatic. Their 'people skills' are outstanding and they have an immense gift both for empathy and for perceiving the feelings and emotions of others. They are very open towards other people, with a genuine interest in their problems and a sincere eagerness to help. With their highly developed intuition and perceptiveness, they are able to divine other people's thoughts, intentions and motives and are also quick to spot problems in interpersonal relationships. Being people of compromise and endowed with the gift of persuasion, they have the ability to build understanding and play an instrumental part in finding solutions which are favourable to all concerned. They are quick-witted, courteous and full of humour.

Counsellors are also excellent conversationalists, with the rare skill of listening to other people and the ability to elicit the best in them, spotting the potential and possibilities that have gone unremarked by others. Talking to *counsellors* inspires people to act, motivates them, lifts their spirits and sets them believing in their own powers. *Counsellors* also have a natural gift for drawing others to them; they are sought-after friends and colleagues. Their charm, warmth and sincerity, their natural attitude of acceptance and their wide range of interests mean that others enjoy being in their company, which gives them a sense of worth and a feeling of being appreciated. They are also natural leaders; where they go, others will follow, infected by their vision and faith that the venture will succeed.

Potential weaknesses

Counsellors are characterised by an extreme optimism and idealism. They usually see reality through rose-tinted glasses and have a tendency to marginalise negative occurrences, limitations and dangers; indeed, they might well fail to spot them at all. They quite often lose touch with reality as far as their ideas are concerned and are liable to subordinate their entire life to accomplishing one ruling notion, a course of action which may well narrow their world and cramp their perceptions. They can be critical and suspicious of opinions and viewpoints which diverge significantly from their own. With their inclination to do too much for others and even, at times, to manipulate them, they can also be overprotective or invasive.

Counsellors cope very badly with situations of conflict and have an exceptionally low threshold of tolerance for criticism levelled at them by others. They often prefer to keep quiet about their troubles or someone else's inappropriate behaviour rather than engage in a difficult conversation about the problem. They will do everything within their power to avoid unpleasant situations and their tendency to throw in the towel prematurely, yield and give up the fight for their own rights may manifest itself as a result. Ending destructive and toxic relationships is also something which frequently causes them difficulty. They have little appreciation for their own achievements and play down their role in successes; on the other hand, they are inclined to pin the blame for failures on themselves. They can have problems with accommodating themselves to socially accepted norms and conventions.

As a rule, *counsellors* are rather inflexible and find situations demanding improvisation hard to handle. They also have difficulty in making decisions on the basis of purely rational and logical premises, without reference to the social context. The awareness that a given decision may have an unfavourable impact on the lives of other people will often leave them paralysed and render them incapable of assessing a situation coolly and taking whatever action might be essential. The problems they sometimes have with carrying out objective evaluations stem from the same cause. Their sensitivity to the opinions and appraisals of others makes it difficult for them to function in an unfriendly environment and even more of a struggle in an outright hostile one. They incline towards perfectionism and this can reduce the efficacy of their activities, since they may well spend time improving things which suffice as they are. In general, they devote too little time to reflecting on their own lives and priorities and, in focusing on other people, they often forget about their own needs.

Similar personality types:

- the Enthusiast
- the Mentor
- the Idealist

Statistical data:

- *counsellors* constitute between three and five per cent of the global community
- women predominate among *counsellors* (80 per cent)
- France is an example of a nation corresponding to the *counsellor's* profile[5]

Find out more!

The Counsellor. Your Guide to the ENFJ Personality Type by Jaroslaw Jankowski

The Director (ENTJ)

Life motto: *I'll tell you what you need to do.*

Directors are independent, active and decisive. Rational, logical and creative, when they analyse problems they look at the wider picture and are able to foresee the future consequences of human activities. They are characterised by optimism and a healthy sense of their own worth and are

---

[5] What this means is not that all the residents of France fall within this personality type, but that French society as a whole possesses a great many of the character traits typical of the *counsellor*.

capable of transforming theoretical concepts into concrete, practical plans of action.

Visionaries, mentors and organisers, *directors* possess natural leadership skills. Their powerful personalities and direct and critical style can often have an intimidating effect, causing them problems in their interpersonal relationships.

The *director's* four natural inclinations:

- source of life energy: the exterior world
- mode of assimilating information: intuition
- decision-making mode: the mind
- lifestyle: organised

Potential strengths

Directors have a healthy sense of their own worth and possess natural leadership skills. Capable of firing others with optimism and faith in their success, they themselves brim with energy, enthusiasm for work and the ability to put their whole heart into accomplishing tasks they believe in. Their vision gives them energy and they are thus able to work extremely hard in order to accomplish it. They are characterised by a positive attitude to tasks and problems, being well aware of the potential difficulties but believing that they will succeed in meeting the challenge. With their serious approach to their responsibilities, one thing is certain: once they take on a job, they will see it through to the end. Fresh concepts and ideas interest them and they are open to new solutions, possessing the ability to assimilate them and apply them when accomplishing their own tasks.

Independent, active and creative, they have the ability to transform theoretical and general concepts into concrete plans of action. They approach their work very seriously and expect the same of others. Their focus is on the merits of the matter and they refuse to allow less crucial aspects to distract them. When analysing facts and data, they are cool and objective, giving emotion and bias short shrift. They are able to manage money and other resources effectively and efficiently and are well-organised and extremely hard-working, as well as being direct and straightforward; no one will ever need to spend time wondering what their opinion on a given topic might be. *Directors* say what they think. They are good oral communicators and public speaking and debate pose no major problems for them.

By nature, they are interested in self-development, acquiring knowledge and self-improvement in various areas of their lives. With their powerful, assertive personality, they cope well in difficult situations of conflict and are capable of putting an end to friendships and acquaintanceships if they become uncomfortable or destructive. They are open to constructive criticism. Given their love of order, they make superb organisers, as well as excelling in orchestrating the work of others, having a flair for creating systems which function effectively and efficiently and being good strategists, with the ability to define priorities with pinpoint accuracy.

Potential weaknesses

Directors pursue confrontation. Their love of tough polemics and dispute means that they are seen as difficult and critical conversationalists, while their powerful personalities often have an intimidating effect on others and can even arouse anxieties and fears. When they argue a point with other people, they strive to prove that they are absolutely right and completely 'wipe the floor' with their opponents; rarely will they be able to admit that someone who holds a different view could be right, even if only in part. They have difficulty in understanding the needs of others when they differ from their own and, by their very nature, are insensitive to other people's feelings and reactions. Expressing their own feelings and emotions comes just as hard to them and they are at rather a loss in situations demanding that they read those of others. They fare no better when it comes to listening, and have a tendency to criticise any opinion whatsoever if it fails to concur with their own point of view.

Highly demanding of themselves, they are no more sparing in the high standards they require others to meet, even though they generally set the benchmark too high for many. When they call other people's attention to wastefulness, perfunctoriness or other oversights, they are often extremely severe and can even be harsh to the point of roughness. At the same time, they are very stinting in their praise when things are going well, setting no store by positive reinforcement in the form of encouragement, approval and rewards. Seizing the initiative comes naturally to them and they are reluctant to share responsibility with others, as well as displaying a frequent tendency to make premature and ill-considered decisions. In extreme cases, their pursuit of authority can see them acting dogmatically and high-handedly towards those they seek to oversee; on occasion, they may well even humiliate them. When they find themselves in stressful situations, they are liable to explode in anger and manifest other forms of aggressive behaviour. They may also endeavour to relieve their tension by overeating or abusing alcohol.

The dogmatism and extremely rational approach to life exhibited by directors, together with their inability to identify other people's needs, are all characteristics which often cause them problems and can lead to a specific form of social isolation, whereby they are highly valued at work but have no friends to speak of. With no real grasp as to why this should be, they will sometimes begin to suspect other people of wishing them ill or conspiring against them. Those who are either incapable of adapting to their ideas and plans or have no wish to do so are another frequent source of frustration to them.

Similar personality types:

- the Innovator
- the Strategist
- the Logician

Statistical data:

- *directors* constitute between two and five per cent of the global community
- men predominate among *directors* (70 per cent)
- Holland is an example of a nation corresponding to the *director's* profile[6]

Find out more!

The Director. Your Guide to the ENTJ Personality Type by Jaroslaw Jankowski

The Enthusiast (ENFP)

Life motto: *We'll manage!*

Enthusiasts are energetic, enthusiastic and optimistic. Capable of enjoying life and looking ahead to the future, they are dynamic, quick-witted and creative. They have a liking for people in general, value honest and genuine relationships and are warm, sincere and emotional. Criticism is something they handle badly. With their gift for empathy and ability to perceive people's needs, feelings and motives, they both inspire others and infect them with their own enthusiasm.

---

[6] What this means is not that all the residents of Holland fall within this personality type, but that Dutch society as a whole possesses a great many of the character traits typical of the *director*.

They love to be at the centre of events and are flexible and capable of improvising. Their inclination leads towards idealistic notions. Being easily distracted, they have problems with seeing things through to the end.

The *enthusiast's* four natural inclinations:

- source of life energy: the exterior world
- mode of assimilating information: intuition
- decision-making mode: the heart
- lifestyle: spontaneous

Potential strengths

Enthusiasts are energetic and optimistic. With their positive attitude to other people and sensitivity to their needs, they emanate warmth and sincerity. As a result, they draw others to themselves naturally and people feel good in their company. They have the ability to read human emotions, feelings and motives, obvious and hidden alike, and are quick to discern who they are dealing with. Their intuition is superb and they display an uncanny tact and 'feel' for others in their interpersonal relationships, knowing exactly how to behave in a given situation and having the ability to build compromises. They are tolerant and accept others, respecting their freedom and independence.

Being flexible and possessing the ability to improvise, they cope extremely well with change and respond rapidly to new circumstances. Versatile, nimble-witted and creative, they are quick to assimilate complex concepts and abstract theories. Their oral communication skills are excellent and they are able to express their own thoughts clearly, as well as having impressive powers of persuasion. They are unperturbed by obstacles and setbacks and have no fear of experiments or innovative methods for solving problems. Their thinking is global; they are able to identify the connections between disparate phenomena and look at the bigger picture when considering problems. They have natural leadership skills and are capable of motivating and inspiring people, as well as infecting them with their optimism and faith in their success, drawing out the best in them and helping them to make the most of their potential. Accepting help from others and availing themselves of their experience also present them with no problems.

Potential weaknesses

Enthusiasts often have trouble with determining their priorities and focusing on carrying out their tasks. As a rule, they launch into a job enthusiastically, but are easily distracted and seeing it through to the end is something of a challenge to them. They may well fail to keep their word or meet deadlines and have a tendency to put off doing what has to be done. Managing their time is another problem area for them, as is planning, and they also struggle mightily with repetitive, everyday activities and routine duties in both their private and their working lives. Be it cleaning and shopping or be it compiling reports and accounts, their efforts, such as they are, will probably be dismal.

They are unable to appreciate constructive criticism or benefit from it and will normally perceive it as an attack on themselves personally or an attempt to discredit their values. Being highly dependent on the opinions of others, they cope very badly with unflattering comments and cutting remarks and will also go to any lengths to avoid conflicts and disagreeable conversations, preferring, on the whole, to keep quiet about a problem rather than confront it.

Voicing critical opinions and calling other people's attention to shortcomings or inappropriate behaviour is difficult for them and they tend to clamp the lid down on their negative emotions. In focusing on other people's needs, they often forget about their own, and since they incline towards being over-trusting they will sometimes be used by others. With their enthusiasm and propensity for viewing the world through rose-tinted glasses, they can lose touch with reality on occasion, fail to view potential threats seriously enough and display a tendency to take excessive risks.

Similar personality types:

- the Counsellor
- the Idealist
- the Mentor

Statistical data:

- *enthusiasts* constitute between five and eight per cent of the global community
- women predominate among *enthusiasts* (60 per cent)
- Italy is an example of a nation corresponding to the *enthusiast's* profile[7]

Find out more!

The Enthusiast. Your Guide to the ENFP Personality Type by Jaroslaw Jankowski

The Idealist (INFP)

Life motto: *We CAN live differently.*

Idealists are sensitive, loyal, and creative. Living in accordance with the values they hold is of immense importance to them and they both manifest an interest in the reality of the spirit and delve deeply into the mysteries of life. Wrapped up in the world's problems and open to the needs of other people, they prize harmony and balance.

---

[7] What this means is not that all the residents of Italy fall within this personality type, but that Italian society as a whole possesses a great many of the character traits typical of the *enthusiast*.

Idealists are romantic; not only are they able to show love, but they also need warmth and affection themselves. With their outstanding ability to read other people's feelings and emotions, they build healthy, profound and enduring relationships. They feel that they are on very shaky ground in situations of conflict and have no real resistance to stress and criticism.

The *idealist's* four natural inclinations:

- source of life energy: the interior world
- mode of assimilating information: intuition
- decision-making mode: the heart
- lifestyle: spontaneous

Potential strengths

Idealists possess extraordinary warmth and are happy to turn it to 'warming' others. By nature sensitive and caring, they have the ability to identify other people's needs. They are alert to any and every manifestation of injustice and seek to act on behalf of those who are wronged, used or abused. Their stable system of values, uncommon empathy and sincere interest in the fate of others predispose them to acting for the social good. Extremely faithful and loyal, they are able to build profound, stable and enduring relationships. At the same time, they neither impose themselves on other people nor restrict them. On the contrary, they bestow their trust on them and provide them with the space to develop. Being remarkably flexible, they cope extremely well with change.

Their characteristic tolerance and openness to others extends to those whom the majority of society has rejected, and they will find positive potential and good in everyone. With their uncanny gift of empathy, they are able to support other people, giving them heart and faith in their own powers. They are also superb listeners, perceiving the feelings and motives of others. Their skills include the ability to build compromise and mutual agreement, leaving everyone involved with a sense of satisfaction and the conviction that they have succeeded in achieving what they wanted. They have no difficulty in digesting complex theories and concepts and, at one and the same time, are highly creative and open to spiritual and artistic experiences. Indeed, they themselves are often artistically gifted. They are also capable of expressing their thoughts, particularly in writing.

Potential weaknesses

Idealists have a very low threshold of immunity to criticism, especially when it comes from those close to them. Even minor disapproving comments or gently caustic jokes can undermine their faith in themselves and cause them immense pain. Indeed, they will sometimes perceive critical allusions even when none are being made. Their tremendous loyalty and attachment to people means that they will frequently have problems with putting an end to harmful or toxic relationships. Expressing critical opinions and calling other people's attention to shortcomings also comes hard to them and they will sometimes even struggle to present their own point of view. When forced to address an issue critically, they will often tread so carefully that the person or people they are talking to will have difficulty in understanding what it is that they are actually trying to say. They cope extremely badly with situations of conflict and may respond by behaving irrationally or making sudden, ill-considered decisions.

The severity of their self-appraisal and their acute need for affirmation and positive reinforcement from others impedes their ability to function in neutral or cold environments, a situation which is only magnified in situations of open disapproval. They are incapable of keeping a cool head in stressful circumstances and can also be subject to excessive emotional swings. Although their ideas are highly creative, they can sometimes be unrealistic, since they often fail to take into account the limitations and imperfections present in the world, with the human fallibility factor being one such instance. They have a tendency to treat opinions which oppose their own as an attack on themselves and their values and, when it comes to new information, they are inclined only to take it on board if it concurs with their views; should it threaten their outlook, they might well suppress it entirely. This approach will sometimes lead them to isolate themselves and shut themselves off in their own world.

Similar personality types:

- the Mentor
- the Enthusiast
- the Counsellor

Statistical data:

- *idealists* constitute between one and four per cent of the global community
- women predominate among *idealists* (60 per cent)
- Thailand is an example of a nation corresponding to the *idealist's* profile[8]

Find out more!

The Idealist. Your Guide to the INFP Personality Type by Jaroslaw Jankowski

---

[8] What this means is not that all the residents of Thailand fall within this personality type, but that Thai society as a whole possesses a great many of the character traits typical of the *idealist.*

The Innovator (ENTP)

Life motto: *How about trying a different approach…?*

Innovators are inventive, original and independent. Optimistic, energetic and enterprising, they are people of action who love being at the centre of events and solving 'insoluble' problems. Their thoughts are turned to the future and they are curious about the world and visionary by nature. Open to new concepts and ideas, they enjoy new experiences and experiments and have the ability to identify the connections between separate events.

Innovators are spontaneous, communicative and self-assured. However, they tend to overestimate their own possibilities and have problems with seeing things through to the end. They are also inclined to be impatient and to take risks.

The *innovator's* four natural inclinations:

- source of life energy: the exterior world
- mode of assimilating information: intuition
- decision-making mode: the mind
- lifestyle: spontaneous

Potential strengths

Innovators are creative, optimistic and energetic, with the ability both to fire others with enthusiasm and faith in their success and to stir them into action. Nimble-minded, they are logical, rational and insusceptible to manipulation by others. Assimilating complex concepts and theories presents them with no problems. They have a natural curiosity about the world and are able to understand the phenomena which occur in it and the mechanisms driving people's behaviour, to identify the connections and relationships between different events and to look at problems from various angles. When opportunities and possibilities emerge, *innovators* are quicker than most to spot them, just as they are to foresee potential, future dangers.

Enterprising by nature, they like new concepts and pioneering ideas and will readily reach for innovative solutions and methods. Being exceptionally creative and bold, they are able to solve problems in unconventional, original ways and they have no fear of experimenting. They are always happy to learn something new and undertake fresh challenges, enjoy solving complex problems and are not afraid to take risks. Extremely flexible and capable of adapting to new circumstances, they enjoy both the company of others and working in a group. In general, they possess outstanding communication skills, being capable of expressing their thoughts and voicing their opinions clearly and comprehensibly. Neither criticism nor confrontation frightens them and they cope well in difficult, conflict situations. They strive for self-improvement and are always willing to help others to develop.

Potential weaknesses

With their love of change and experiment, pursuit of the new and focus on the latest and most powerful stimuli, *innovators* have far less difficulty in beginning something than they do in seeing it through to the end. They are also easily distracted and their enthusiasm for the tasks they have started vanishes when new problems and challenges appear on the horizon. This means that they drop numerous fascinating ideas at the conceptual stage without even trying to implement them in reality. They also struggle with organising their time, applying self-discipline, making decisions, keeping promises and sticking to deadlines. Defining priorities and then bringing their activities in line with them is also problematic for them. They cope badly with tasks which require them to adhere to strict procedures and follow instructions to the letter.

Another problem which frequently crops up among *innovators* is their impatience with less experienced people who need guidelines, prompting and pointers. Their boldness and unwavering faith that they will succeed may well lead to their making overly risky moves and employing excessively radical solutions. They are liable to overestimate their own possibilities and disregard their limitations. Both their inability to perceive the emotions and feelings of others and the difficulty they have in expressing their own can give rise to problems in their relationships with those closest to them. At the same time, with their confrontational approach, critical comments, general determination to have things their own way and love of dispute and polemic, they are likely to hurt and discourage more sensitive people and may even frighten them away.

Similar personality types:

- the Director
- the Logician
- the Strategist

Statistical data:

- *innovators* constitute between three and five per cent of the global community
- men predominate among *innovators* (70 per cent)
- Israel is an example of a nation corresponding to the *innovator's* profile[9]

Find out more!

The Innovator. Your Guide to the ENTP Personality Type by Jaroslaw Jankowski

---

[9] What this means is not that all the residents of Israel fall within this personality type, but that Israeli society as a whole possesses a great many of the character traits typical of the *innovator*.

The Inspector (ISTJ)

Life motto: *Duty first.*

Inspectors are people who can always be counted on. Well-mannered, punctual, reliable, conscientious and responsible, when they give their word, they keep it. Being analytical, methodical, systematic and logical by nature, they tend be seen as serious, cold and reserved. They prize calm, stability and order, have no fondness for change and like clear principles and concrete rules.

Inspectors are hard-working, persevering and capable of seeing things through to the end. As perfectionists, they try to exercise control over everything within their sphere and are sparing in their praise. They also underrate the importance of other people's feelings and emotions.

The *inspector's* four natural inclinations:

- source of life energy: the interior world
- mode of assimilating information: via the senses
- decision-making mode: the mind
- lifestyle: organised

Potential strengths

Inspectors love order and hold tradition and rules in great respect. True to their word, loyal and steadfast, they take their responsibilities extremely seriously, care for their families and are ready to devote themselves to those closest to them. Their reliability, punctuality and ability to stick to a deadline all arouse the respect of others. Quick to spot gaps, errors and oversights, they are hard-working to a fault and always see things through to the end, without allowing obstacles to discourage them – an attitude which means that they usually attain their goals. They are capable of performing work which demands that they adhere to a host of procedures, process large quantities of data and carry out myriad routine activities.

Sharing their knowledge and experience with other people and helping them to resolve concrete problems is something they do willingly. Capable of expressing their thoughts and voicing their opinions clearly and matter-of-factly, they have little difficulty in convincing others that they are right. They cope well in situations of conflict and are open to constructive criticism from other people; it neither upsets them nor do they see it as a personal attack. At the same time, they are not easily dissuaded from their own views and opinions. When the need arises, they are able to discipline others and call their attention to shortcomings without feeling the need to tread delicately. They are excellent at managing money.

Potential weaknesses

Reading the feelings of others and perceiving their emotional needs is problematic for *inspectors*. Sparing in their praise, they also struggle when it comes to expressing love and affection. Their colleagues and those closest to them are often wearied by their driving urge to set everything in their sphere in order and then control it.

Assuming that they are always right, they tend to be premature in ruling out alternative solutions and other points of view. Looking at problems from a wider perspective and understanding opinions which differ from their own is also difficult for them and they will often dismiss other people's views in advance, without even trying to hear them out. When confronted by a problem, they have a tendency to blame others.

They cope badly with change and new situations. Their natural predilection for keeping strictly to guidelines, instructions and procedures can prove limiting in numerous circumstances, while their inclination to rely on previous experience and tried and tested solutions becomes an obstacle when they encounter new tasks requiring an approach which departs from the norm.

Similar personality types:

- the Practitioner
- the Administrator
- the Animator

Statistical data:

- *inspectors* constitute between six and ten per cent of the global community
- men predominate among *inspectors* (60 per cent)
- Switzerland is an example of a nation corresponding to the *inspector's* profile[10]

Find out more!

The Inspector. Your Guide to the ISTJ Personality Type by Jaroslaw Jankowski

The Logician (INTP)

Life motto: *Above all else, seek to discover the truths about the world.*

Logicians are original, resourceful and creative. With a love for solving problems of a theoretical nature, they are analytical, quick-witted, enthusiastically disposed towards new concepts and have the ability to connect individual phenomena, educing general rules and theories from them. Logical, exact and inquiring, they are quick to spot incoherence and inconsistency.

---

[10] What this means is not that all the residents of Switzerland fall within this personality type, but that Swiss society as a whole possesses a great many of the character traits typical of the *inspector*.

Logicians are independent, sceptical of existing solutions and authorities, tolerant and open to new challenges. When immersed in thought, they will sometimes lose touch with the outside world.

The *logician's* four natural inclinations:

- source of life energy: the interior world
- mode of assimilating information: intuition
- decision-making mode: the mind
- lifestyle: spontaneous

Potential strengths

Logicians are extraordinarily intelligent, creative and inventive, with the ability to connect disparate facts and experiences and build comprehensive and cohesive systems from them. Unconventional and original, their attitude towards new concepts and ideas is an enthusiastic one. Their concentration skills are extraordinary and they are impossible to distract; dragging them away from a task they deem important is a struggle, since they are more than capable of turning their entire energy towards solving whatever problem is currently engaging them. They are characterised by their high level of intellectual independence and other people's opinions make no major impression on them. If a point of view seems to them to be logically lacking in cohesion and irrational, they will discard it without regard for whether or not a recognised authority stands behind it or the majority subscribe to it.

They have the ability to make excellent use of their experiences, successes and failures alike. By nature persevering, they will usually set themselves a high benchmark and, as a result, they frequently become genuine experts in the fields they are involved in. Perfectly at home in the world of abstract theories and complex concepts, they have the gifts of assimilating them and of logical, rational thinking, along with a natural talent for mathematics and the ability to formulate their thoughts precisely and succinctly. They are quick to spot any kind of incoherence, inconsistency or logical discrepancy; at the same time, their extraordinary precision and logicality go hand in hand with their tolerance, flexibility and open-mindedness. They accord other people freedom and independence, are able to make decisions quickly and have no problem handling criticism from others.

Potential weaknesses

Logicians are extremely logical, but their logic can be subjective and selective, since they have a tendency to focus on information which is connected to their current object of interest or constitutes a confirmation of their opinions and experience. At the same time, they might well discard arguments and findings which either go against their own experience or are not grounded in logic, and they are capable of simply ignoring people who live and perceive the world in a way different from their own. They frequently involve themselves solely in things which suit their inclinations and interest them, a tendency which can eventually limit their experiences and contact with others. Indeed, it might even lead to a form of self-isolation.

Logicians find voicing their own emotions challenging. They also struggle with perceiving the emotional needs of others and may well hurt them without the slightest awareness that they have done so. Sometimes unreliable, unpunctual, forgetful and absent-minded, they cope badly with everyday, routine activities. Implementing theoretical concepts in practice is also something they have little aptitude for. In stressful situations, they are likely to react to stimuli in ways which are out of all proportion and lose their sense of self-assurance. Deprived of the possibility of engaging in what fascinates them, they may begin to construct a negatively critical attitude towards the world around them. As it develops, it becomes manifest in the form of questioning the sincere intentions of others, correcting them to an abnormal extent and criticising anything and everything which goes against their own point of view.

Similar personality types:

- the Strategist
- the Innovator
- the Director

Statistical data:

- *logicians* constitute between two and three per cent of the global community;
- men predominate among *logicians* (80 per cent)
- India is an example of a nation corresponding to the *logician's* profile[11]

Find out more!

The Logician. Your Guide to the INTP Personality Type by Jaroslaw Jankowski

The Mentor (INFJ)

Life motto: ***The world CAN be a better place!***

Mentors are creative and sensitive. With their gaze fixed firmly on the future, they spot opportunities and potential imperceptible to others. Idealists and visionaries, they are geared towards helping people and are conscientious, responsible and, at one and the same time, courteous, caring and friendly. They strive to understand the mechanisms

---

[11] What this means is not that all the residents of India fall within this personality type, but that Indian society as a whole possesses a great many of the character traits typical of the *logician.*

governing the world and view problems from a wide perspective.

Superb listeners and observers, *mentors* are characterised by their extraordinary empathy, intuition and trust of people and are capable of reading the feelings and emotions of others. They find criticism and conflict difficult to bear and can come across as enigmatic.

The *mentor's* four natural inclinations:

- source of life energy: the interior world
- mode of assimilating information: intuition
- decision-making mode: the heart
- lifestyle: organised

Potential strengths

Mentors perceive things which are far from evident to others, seeing the connections between disparate events and repeated patterns of behaviour. When working to solve problems, they analyse the situation from various angles and different perspectives and have the ability to look ahead and identify future potential, possibilities and dangers. Their ideas are highly creative and unconventional and they have an excellent grasp of complex theories and abstract concepts.

They forge natural, sincere and profound interpersonal relationships, being genuinely interested in other people and their problems and sensitive to their feelings and needs. Characterised by their extraordinary intuition, empathy and natural warm-heartedness, they are splendid observers and listeners, capable of reading the feelings and emotions of others, inspiring them to discover and make the most of their potential and motivating them to take responsibility for their own lives.

Mentors strive for perfection and are able to penetrate beneath the surface of problems and identify their essence. When they see the sense of their work, they are capable of focusing on the task or matter in hand and are ready to make numerous sacrifices in devoting themselves to it. Conscientious and responsible, they treat any and every task they undertake seriously and are incapable of consciously working to anything less than their full ability. Indeed, given their desire to see everyone make the most of their potential and talents, they are extremely demanding of themselves and others alike. As past masters of the spoken and written word, they are able to express their thoughts clearly and comprehensibly.

Potential weaknesses

Mentors' idealism means that they often have trouble functioning in the real world and can be rather unfocused; for instance, when discussing a problem, they may well diverge from the matter in hand, drifting into considerations of a more general nature. They also struggle with everyday, routine activities and are inclined to forget details.

Their expectations of others can be unrealistic and may fail to make allowances for people's natural limitations, a tendency which often gives the impression that they are impossible to satisfy. As a rule, they assume that they are right, often not even offering an explanation of the basis for that conviction. They are also prone to dismissing other people's views in advance, without trying to hear them out. Their multilayered perception of reality often causes them to reflect on the rightness of the road they have chosen and the decisions they have made. They are frequently at a loss in situations requiring improvisation or rapid decisions.

Sharing their problems with others and accepting their help comes hard to them, as does coping in situations of conflict. They handle criticism very badly, often taking it as a personal attack and they respond poorly to stress, which drives them into a state of internal tension, frequently triggering somatic symptoms and depriving them of their faith in their own capabilities; indeed, at times, they will even turn to using substances.

Mentors are not only highly sensitive and easily hurt, but can also struggle to forgive, and may well go on nursing their injuries for a long time.

Similar personality types:

- the Idealist
- the Counsellor
- the Enthusiast

Statistical data:

- *mentors* constitute one per cent of the global community and are the most rarely occurring of the sixteen personality types
- women predominate among *mentors* (80 per cent)
- Norway is an example of a nation corresponding to the *mentor's* profile[12]

Find out more!

The Mentor. Your Guide to the INFJ Personality Type by Jaroslaw Jankowski

The Practitioner (ISTP)

Life motto: *Actions speak louder than words.*

Practitioners are optimistic and spontaneous, with a positive approach to life. Reserved and independent, they hold true to their personal convictions and view external principles and norms with scepticism. They find abstract concepts and

---

[12] What this means is not that all the residents of Norway fall within this personality type, but that Norwegian society as a whole possesses a great many of the character traits typical of the *mentor*.

solutions for the future tiresome and would far rather roll up their sleeves and get to work on solving tangible and concrete problems.

Adapting well to new places and situations, they enjoy fresh challenges and risks and are capable of keeping a cool head in the face of threats and danger. Their general reticence and extreme reserve when it comes to expressing their opinions mean that other people may often find them impenetrable.

The *practitioner's* four natural inclinations:

- source of life energy: the interior world
- mode of assimilating information: via the senses
- decision-making mode: the mind
- lifestyle: spontaneous

Potential strengths

Practitioners are spontaneous, flexible and tolerant. As excellent listeners and observers, they spot details which escape the notice of others, using the information they acquire to build an internal database unique to themselves and then applying it to solving concrete problems. Practical by nature, they have inbuilt manual and technical skills. They are self-assured, enthusiastic and optimism is their middle name. Their approach to life is positive ... *practitioners* have the ability to enjoy every moment. Change holds no fear for them and they would always rather be up and doing. When those close to them need their practical assistance, they will spare neither time nor energy in providing it.

No matter what, *practitioners* will stand firm by their convictions, remaining insusceptible to external pressure. They can handle criticism and have no trouble in expressing it themselves or calling other people's attention to shortcomings. Capable of making decisions on the basis of partial data and acting under conditions of increased risk, they cope extremely well in situations of threat and danger, crises and rapidly shifting circumstances. When others are overcome by emotion, *practitioners* keep a cool head, making objective and rational decisions. They are unafraid of bold moves and risk, a character trait which also means that they are capable of ending toxic and destructive relationships.

Potential weaknesses

The inability to express their feelings is one of the greatest weaknesses which *practitioners* face, along with their insensitivity to the emotional needs of others, an aspect of their natures which can mean that they cause hurt without even being aware of it. Their reticence may also be a source of problems, as may the fact that they have little grasp of how to suit their mode of communication to the moment. Their loathing of any kind of supervision or oversight can lead to their becoming uniquely obsessive as regards their privacy and even to their self-isolation.

Coping with long-term tasks and strategic planning comes hard to *practitioners*, since they have difficulty in seeing the wider perspective, the long-term effects of their decisions and the connections between disparate facts and phenomena, to say nothing of assimilating complex, abstract theories. Given that they are quick to grow bored, they also find focusing on one thing for an extended period an uphill struggle and are easily distracted. As such, they tend to find starting something far easier than following it through to the end.

Inclined to dismiss anything that conflicts with their own experience, they surround themselves with people who share their interests and views, a *modus operandi* which can lead to their developing their own alternative vision of the world. Despite their openness to new knowledge and experiment in the fields which interest them, they themselves rarely step beyond the areas that they are already familiar with.

Similar personality types:

- the Inspector
- the Animator
- the Administrator

Statistical data:

- *practitioners* constitute between six and nine per cent of the global community
- men predominate among *practitioners* (60 per cent)
- Singapore is an example of a nation corresponding to the *practitioner's* profile[13]

Find out more!

The Practitioner. Your Guide to the ISTP Personality Type by Jaroslaw Jankowski

The Presenter (ESFP)

Life motto: *Now is the perfect moment!*

Presenters are optimistic, energetic and outgoing, with the ability to enjoy life and have fun to the full. Practical, flexible and spontaneous at one and the same time, they enjoy change and new experiences, coping badly with solitude, stagnation and routine.

With their liking for being at the centre of attention, they are natural-born actors and their speaking abilities arouse the interest and enthusiasm of their listeners. Focused as they are on the present moment, they will sometimes lose

---

[13] What this means is not that all the residents of Singapore fall within this personality type, but that Singaporean society as a whole possesses a great many of the character traits typical of the *practitioner*.

sight of their long-term aims and can also have problems with foreseeing the consequences of their actions.

The *presenter's* four natural inclinations:

- source of life energy: the exterior world
- mode of assimilating information: via the senses
- decision-making mode: the heart
- lifestyle: spontaneous

Potential strengths

Presenters are enthusiastic, spontaneous and flexible. Capable of reacting rapidly to shifting circumstances and adapting to new conditions, they are practical and learn fast. With their love of experiment and fearless attitude towards risk, they cope well with change and, being optimistic by nature, they are not disheartened by obstacles and difficulties. They also have the ability to enjoy every day and make the most of every moment. Their enthusiasm and optimism is infectious and tends to have a positive impact on others and, when they work as part of a group, they are able both to integrate the team and build comprises. Their interest in other people and concern for their happiness and well-being is genuine, as is their respect for their freedom and individuality. They are always ready to lend a helping hand and, at one and the same time, have no trouble in either accepting assistance from others or in making the most of their experience and advice.

Excellent observers of the world around them and of human emotions and feelings, they are just as skilled at rapidly 'reading' other people. With their outgoing, open nature, they are easy to get to know and, in general, they are sought-after companions. Their optimism and sense of humour draws others to them, while their warm, sincere interest encourages people to confide in them. Their inherent acting skills go hand in hand with a developed artistic and aesthetic sense, and they are natural-born speakers, compères and presenters, endowed with the ability to arouse the interest and enthusiasm of their listeners. Remarkably generous and ready to meet the needs of others, they love not only helping them, but also giving them gifts, offering them a variety of attractions, preparing surprises for them and finding ways for them to while away the time pleasantly – all of which is helped by their ability to adapt to whatever the circumstances may currently be.

Potential weaknesses

Presenters face an uphill struggle when it comes to extending their thoughts beyond the here and now, carrying out jobs which demand that they envisage what may happen in the future or sacrifice current pleasures for the sake of distant benefits. Tasks which require lengthy focus and concentration or require them to work alone are a source of misery to them, particularly when the outcome of their efforts will only become visible with time. They also view the world of abstract concepts and complex theories as unmapped and impenetrable territory and are inclined both to ignore anything which cannot be turned into practical action and to over-simplify, or quite often, even to trivialise problems. To *presenters*, the ideal solution will always be one which is straightforward, fast and requires nothing much in the way of penetrating reflection. While this approach enables them to get rid of a problem that has arisen – and thus turn their energies to more pleasant pursuits – it rarely affords them an understanding of the underlying causes. By the same token, their focus on fun, pleasure and entertainment means that they sometimes fail to discern life's more profound dimensions.

Understanding diverse standpoints and looking at a situation or issue through the eyes of others can also be problematic for *presenters,* and they often fear opinions and points of view which diverge significantly from their own. They find criticism levelled at them by other people extremely hard to take, treating it as either an attack or a manifestation of spitefulness and, in general, they are incapable of putting it to constructive use. This works both ways, since they themselves find it equally difficult to express a critical opinion. When faced with problems, unpleasant situations or conflict, *presenters* tend to turn tail and run. As a rule, they do no better when it comes to routine tasks and repetitive activities and, in general, managing finances is not one of their strengths either.

Similar personality types:

- the Advocate
- the Artist
- the Protector

Statistical data:

- *presenters* constitute between eight and thirteen per cent of the global community
- women predominate among *presenters* (60 per cent)
- Brazil is an example of a nation corresponding to the *presenter's* profile[14]

Find out more!

The Presenter. Your Guide to the ESFP Personality Type by Jaroslaw Jankowski

---

[14] What this means is not that all the residents of Brazil fall within this personality type, but that Brazilian society as a whole possesses a great many of the character traits typical of the *presenter*.

The Protector (ISFJ)

Life motto: *Your happiness matters to me.*

Protectors are sincere, warm-hearted, unassuming, trustworthy and extraordinarily loyal. With their ability to perceive people's needs and their desire to help them, they will always put others first. Practical, well-organised and gifted with both an eye and a memory for detail, they are responsible, hard-working, patient, persevering and capable of seeing things through to the end.

Protectors set great store by tranquillity, stability and friendly relations with others and are skilled at building bridges between people. By the same token, they find conflict and criticism difficult to bear. Given their powerful sense of duty and their constant readiness to come to the aid of others, they can end up being used by people.

The *protector's* four natural inclinations:

- source of life energy: the interior world
- mode of assimilating information: via the senses
- decision-making mode: the heart
- lifestyle: organised

Potential strengths

Protectors are uncommonly loyal and take their responsibilities extremely seriously. Hard-working, persevering and patient, they are always ready to commit themselves to the full, sparing neither time nor energy in fulfilling their tasks and seeing things through to the end, undiscouraged by obstacles and setbacks. They are open to others, genuinely interested in them and capable of perceiving their feelings, enthusiasms and emotions. Their attitude is friendly and they are discreet, loyal and geared towards the needs of other people, putting them first and giving no real thought to themselves.

Other people feel good in their company, since they are excellent listeners and offer practical and emotional support to those in need of help or caught in the midst of a crisis. Consensus is one of their watchwords; they create a healthy, constructive atmosphere and will always strive to build bridges between people and assist them in reaching a compromise.

Their spatial imagination is as superb as is their sense of practicality. Orderliness comes as naturally to them as breathing, they see nothing tedious about carrying out routine activities and have no difficulty in following complex procedures. Given their natural talent for organisation, their head for detail and their ability to keep in mind the kind of minutiae that escape the notice of others, they make excellent resource managers.

Potential weaknesses

Being oriented towards serving others and rather lacking in assertiveness, *protectors* are sometimes neglectful of their own needs and backward in defending their own interests. Indeed, they often find themselves incapable of articulating their expectations or voicing their opinions, particularly when they veer towards the critical, and are equally as unable to end toxic and damaging relationships. Their tendency to remain silent on thorny subjects and avoid difficult conversations, even when they are essential, renders them vulnerable to deceit, manipulation and being used by others. They struggle just as much with expressing their feelings, which run deep and intense; indeed, their constant suppression of negative emotions will sometimes lead to uncontrolled and destructive explosions.

They find it difficult to cope in fields of activity which are completely new to them and, being rather inflexible, they quickly find themselves completely at sea in situations demanding swift decisions or improvisation and tend to be knocked off their feet by crises. They also have a problem with delegating duties and responsibilities, as well as tendency to do too much for others and help them whether they like it or not.

When it comes to viewing reality, *protectors* frequently struggle to look at the bigger picture. Understanding other people's views when they conflict with their own also comes hard to them; indeed, simply encountering those opinions can cause them deep discomfort. Inclined to perceive their own ideas as exclusively 'right', they are prone to negating anything which goes against their convictions and discarding it prematurely. They have no real mechanisms for handling criticism either, and frequently take unfavourable opinions of their outlook or activities as a personal defeat and a sign that they have disappointed people.

Similar personality types:

- the Artist
- the Advocate
- the Presenter

Statistical data:

- *protectors* constitute between eight and twelve per cent of the global population
- women predominate among *protectors* (70 per cent)
- Sweden is an example of a nation corresponding to the *protector's* profile[15]

Find out more!

The Protector. Your Guide to the ISFJ Personality Type by Jaroslaw Jankowski

---

[15] What this means is not that all the residents of Sweden fall within this personality type, but that Swedish society as a whole possesses a great many of the character traits typical of the *protector*.

The Strategist (INTJ)

Life motto: *I can certainly improve this.*

Strategists are independent and outstandingly individualistic, with an immense seam of inner energy. Creative, inventive and resourceful, others perceive them as competent, self-assured and, at one and the same time, distant and enigmatic. No matter what they turn their attention to, they will always look at the bigger picture and they have a driving urge to improve the world around them and set it in order.

Well-organised, responsible, critical and demanding, they are difficult to knock off balance – and just as hard to please to the full. Reading the emotions and feelings of others is something they find very problematic.

The *strategist's* four natural inclinations:

- source of life energy: the interior world
- mode of assimilating information: intuition
- decision-making mode: the mind
- lifestyle: organised

Potential strengths

Strategists have penetrating minds and spotting things which remain hidden to others is a piece of cake to them. Quick to identify cause-and-effect relationships and repetitive patterns in human behaviour, they are outstanding analysts and strategists, with the ability to look at problems from a wide perspective and find optimal solutions. When a difficult situation arises, they are also able to predict various scenarios for its development. They are highly independent and impervious to criticism, but perfectly capable of changing their opinion when they see the possibility of improving something or identify a better solution. With a tenacious approach to their work, they devote enormous energy to anything that matters to them, an attitude which means that they usually attain their goals.

Inventors by nature, they have the intelligence and ability to comprehend complex theories, a logical mindset, and a persistence which enable them to discover new solutions or put existing ones to use in fresh and creative ways. Endowed with a healthy sense of their own worth, they cope well in situations of conflict and are capable of evaluating issues with a cool eye, objectively and without emotion. They take their responsibilities extremely seriously and are always ready both to learn something new and to work to improve themselves and their relations with other people. However, should the need arise, they are fully capable of freeing themselves from destructive or toxic relationships.

Potential weaknesses

Reading the feelings of others and perceiving their emotional needs is problematic for *strategists*, as is expressing their own. They are often viewed as withdrawn, impervious and given to keeping people at a distance. Their attitude not only creates tension in their contact with others, but frequently hurts them, while they themselves remain oblivious to the fact that they have caused someone pain. By the same token, in situations of conflict, they endeavour to solve the problem by applying logical arguments and appealing to common sense, whilst underrating the importance of other people's feelings and emotions. As a result, they often fail to understand that many an issue can be resolved by offering spiritual support, encouragement and comfort – a sphere in which *strategists* tread gingerly at best. When all these problems accumulate, they can lead to the point where, feeling like outsiders, they will retreat into self-imposed isolation, blaming other people for problems which are actually of their own making.

Their constant striving to improve anything and everything is something that frequently proves wearisome to the other members of their household and their colleagues alike, as do both their self-assurance and their conviction that they are always right. Problems are also triggered by their high, often unrealistic, expectations of others. They have a low threshold of tolerance for other people's weaknesses and review their achievements with a critical eye. In the world seen from their standpoint, there are shortcomings, defects and errors wherever they look. They probe for inconsistencies in other people's reasoning and for gaps in their argumentation, and on many an occasion this will lead them to discard their opinions and suggestions prematurely. Another potential source of problems for *strategists* is their natural leaning towards workaholism and an inability to relax.

Similar personality types:

- the Logician
- the Director
- the Innovator

Statistical data:

- *strategists* constitute between one and two per cent of the global community
- men predominate among *strategists* (80 per cent)
- Finland is an example of a nation corresponding to the *strategist's* profile[16]

Find out more!

The Strategist. Your Guide to the INTJ Personality Type by Jaroslaw Jankowski

---

[16] What this means is not that all the residents of Finland fall within this personality type, but that Finnish society as a whole possesses a great many of the character traits typical of the *strategist*.

Additional Information

The four natural inclinations

1. THE DOMINANT SOURCE OF LIFE ENERGY

    a. THE EXTERIOR WORLD
    People who draw their energy from outside. They need activity and contact with others and find being alone for any length of time hard to bear.

    b. THE INTERIOR WORLD
    People who draw their energy from their inner world. They need quiet and solitude and feel drained when they spend any length of time in a group.

2. THE DOMINANT MODE OF
   ASSIMILATING INFORMATION

    a. VIA THE SENSES
   People who rely on the five senses and
   are persuaded by facts and evidence. They
   have a liking for methods and practices
   which are tried and tested and prefer
   concrete tasks and are realists who trust in
   experience.

    b. VIA INTUITION
   People who rely on the sixth sense and
   are driven by what they 'feel in their
   bones'. They have a liking for innovative
   solutions and problems of a theoretical
   nature and are characterised by a creative
   approach to their tasks and the ability to
   predict.

3. THE DOMINANT DECISION-MAKING
   MODE

    a. THE MIND
   People who are guided by logic and
   objective principles. They are critical and
   direct in expressing their opinions.

    b. THE HEART
   People who are guided by their feelings
   and values. They long for harmony and
   mutual understanding with others.

4. THE DOMINANT LIFESTYLE

    a. ORGANISED
   People who are conscientious and

organised. They value order and like to operate according to plan.

b. SPONTANEOUS
People who are spontaneous and value freedom of action. They live for the moment and have no trouble finding their feet in new situations.

The approximate percentage of each personality type in the world population

Personality Type:	Proportion:
• The Administrator (ESTJ):	10-13%
• The Advocate (ESFJ):	10-13%
• The Animator (ESTP):	6-10%
• The Artist (ISFP):	6-9%
• The Counsellor (ENFJ):	3-5 %
• The Director (ENTJ):	2-5%
• The Enthusiast (ENFP):	5-8%
• The Idealist (INFP):	1-4%
• The Innovator (ENTP):	3-5%
• The Inspector (ISTJ):	6-10%
• The Logician (INTP):	2-3%
• The Mentor (INFJ):	ca. 1%
• The Practitioner (ISTP):	6-9%
• The Presenter (ESFP):	8-13%
• The Protector (ISFJ):	8-12%
• The Strategist (INTJ):	1-2%

The approximate percentage of women and men of each personality type in the world population

Personality Type:	Women / Men:
• The Administrator (ESTJ):	40% / 60%
• The Advocate (ESFJ):	70% / 30%
• The Animator (ESTP):	40% / 60%
• The Artist (ISFP):	60% / 40%
• The Counsellor (ENFJ):	80% / 20%
• The Director (ENTJ):	30% / 70%
• The Enthusiast (ENFP):	60% / 40%
• The Idealist (INFP):	60% / 40%
• The Innovator (ENTP):	30% / 70%
• The Inspector (ISTJ):	40% / 60%
• The Logician (INTP):	20% / 80%
• The Mentor (INFJ):	80% / 20%
• The Practitioner (ISTP):	40% / 60%
• The Presenter (ESFP):	60% / 40%
• The Protector (ISFJ):	70% / 30%
• The Strategist (INTJ):	20% / 80%

Recommended Publications

The ID16™© Personality Types series

by Jaroslaw Jankowski, M.Ed., EMBA

The series consists of sixteen books on individual personality types:

- *The Administrator. Your Guide to the ESTJ Personality Type*
- *The Advocate. Your Guide to the ESFJ Personality Type*
- *The Animator. Your Guide to the ESTP Personality Type*
- *The Artist. Your Guide to the ISFP Personality Type*
- *The Counsellor. Your Guide to the ENFJ Personality Type*
- *The Director. Your Guide to the ENTJ Personality Type*
- *The Enthusiast. Your Guide to the ENFP Personality Type*
- *The Idealist. Your Guide to the INFP Personality Type*
- *The Innovator. Your Guide to the ENTP Personality Type*
- *The Inspector. Your Guide to the ISTJ Personality Type*
- *The Logician. Your Guide to the INTP Personality Type*
- *The Mentor. Your Guide to the INFJ Personality Type*

- *The Practitioner. Your Guide to the ISTP Personality Type*
- *The Presenter. Your Guide to the ESFP Personality Type*
- *The Protector. Your Guide to the ISFJ Personality Type*
- *The Strategist. Your Guide to the INTJ Personality Type*

The series offers a comprehensive description of each of the sixteen types. As you explore them, you will find the answer to a number of crucial questions:

- How do the people who fall within a particular personality type think and what do they feel? How do they make decisions? How do they solve problems? What makes them anxious? What do they fear? What irritates them?

- Which personality types are they happy to encounter on their road through life and which ones do they avoid? What kind of friends, life partners and parents do they make? How are they perceived by others?

- What are their vocational predispositions? What sort of work environments allow them to function most effectively? Which careers best suit their personality type?

- What are their strengths and what do they need to work on? How can they make the most of their potential and avoid pitfalls?

- Which famous people fall within a particular personality type?

- Which nation displays the most features characteristic of a given type?

The books also contain the most essential information about the ID16™© typology.

Bibliography

- Arraj, Tyra & Arraj, James: *Tracking the Elusive Human, Volume 1: A Practical Guide to C.G. Jung's Psychological Types, W.H. Sheldon's Body and Temperament Types and Their Integration*, Inner Growth Books, 1988

- Arraj, James: *Tracking the Elusive Human, Volume 2: An Advanced Guide to the Typological Worlds of C. G. Jung, W.H. Sheldon, Their Integration, and the Biochemical Typology of the Future*, Inner Growth Books, 1990

- Berens, Linda V.; Cooper, Sue A.; Ernst, Linda K.; Martin, Charles R.; Myers, Steve; Nardi, Dario; Pearman, Roger R.; Segal, Marci; Smith, Melissa: *A Quick Guide to the 16 Personality Types in Organizations: Understanding Personality Differences in the Workplace*, Telos Publications, 2002

- Geier, John G. & Dorothy E. Downey: *Energetics of Personality*, Aristos Publishing House, 1989

- Hunsaker, Phillip L. & Anthony J. Alessandra: *The Art of Managing People*, Simon and Schuster, 1986
- Jung, Carl Gustav: *Psychological Types (The Collected Works of C. G. Jung, Vol. 6)*, Princeton University Press, 1976
- Kise, Jane A. G.; Stark, David & Krebs Hirsch, Sandra: *LifeKeys: Discover Who You Are*, Bethany House, 2005
- Kroeger, Otto & Thuesen, Janet: *Type Talk or How to Determine Your Personality Type and Change Your Life*, Delacorte Press, 1988
- Lawrence, Gordon: *People Types and Tiger Stripes*, Center for Applications of Psychological Type, 1993
- Lawrence, Gordon: *Looking at Type and Learning Styles*, Center for Applications of Psychological Type, 1997
- Maddi, Salvatore R.: *Personality Theories: A Comparative Analysis*, Waveland, 2001
- Martin, Charles R.: *Looking at Type: The Fundamentals Using Psychological Type To Understand and Appreciate Ourselves and Others*, Center for Applications of Psychological Type, 2001
- Meier C.A.: Personality: *The Individuation Process in the Light of C. G. Jung's Typology*, Daimon Verlag, 2007
- Pearman, Roger R. & Albritton, Sarah: *I'm Not Crazy, I'm Just Not You: The Real Meaning of the Sixteen Personality Types*, Davies-Black Publishing, 1997
- Segal, Marci: Creativity and Personality Type: *Tools for Understanding and Inspiring the Many Voices of Creativity*, Telos Publications, 2001
- Sharp, Daryl: Personality Type: *Jung's Model of Typology*, Inner City Books, 1987
- Spoto, Angelo: *Jung's Typology in Perspective*, Chiron Publications, 1995
- Tannen, Deborah: *You Just Don't Understand*, William Morrow and Company, 1990

BIBLIOGRAPHY

- Thomas, Jay C. & Segal, Daniel L.: *Comprehensive Handbook of Personality and Psychopathology, Personality and Everyday Functioning*, Wiley, 2005

- Thomson, Lenore: *Personality Type: An Owner's Manual*, Shambhala, 1998

- Tieger, Paul D. & Barron-Tieger Barbara: *Just Your Type: Create the Relationship You've Always Wanted Using the Secrets of Personality Type*, Little, Brown and Company, 2000

- Von Franz, Marie-Louise & Hillman, James: *Lectures on Jung's Typology*, Continuum International Publishing Group, 1971

About the Author

Jaroslaw Jankowski holds a Master of Education degree from Nicolaus Copernicus University in Toruń, Poland and an MBA from the Brennan School of Business at the Dominican University in River Forest, Illinois, USA. The research and development director of an international NGO and an entrepreneur, he is also involved in voluntary work. He is not only committed to promoting knowledge about personality types, but is also the creator of ID16™©, an independent personality typology based on the theory developed by Carl Gustav Jung.

Putting the Reader first.

An Author Campaign Facilitated by ALLi.

15723946R00056

Printed in Great Britain
by Amazon